by SHARON LANGLEY and AMY NATHAN
illustrated by FLOYD COOPER

A RIDE TO REMEMBER

A Civil Rights Story

Abrams Books for Young Readers • New York

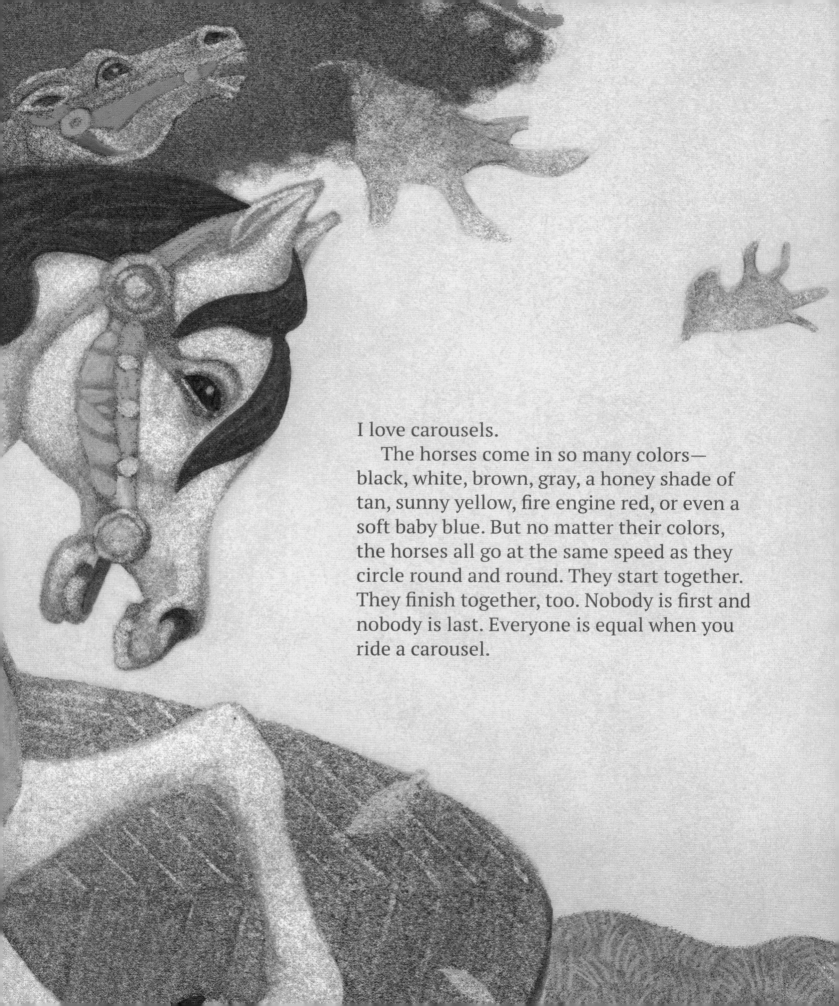

I love carousels.

The horses come in so many colors—black, white, brown, gray, a honey shade of tan, sunny yellow, fire engine red, or even a soft baby blue. But no matter their colors, the horses all go at the same speed as they circle round and round. They start together. They finish together, too. Nobody is first and nobody is last. Everyone is equal when you ride a carousel.

When I was a very little girl, my family lived in Baltimore. Near our house was an amusement park. It was green and grassy, big and beautiful, bright and shiny. There were rides and games, treats and cold drinks at Gwynn Oak Amusement Park—and a carousel, too.

But before I was born, there were no rides or sweets at that park for children like me.

"Was it because kids didn't have money to buy tickets?" I asked Mama.
"No, it wasn't about money," said Mama.
"Or was it because they lived too far away from the park?" I asked.
"That wasn't the problem either," said Daddy.
"Then why?" I wondered aloud.

"It was because of an unfair rule the park had," Daddy explained. "The rule said that African Americans couldn't go on any of the rides."

"Could we go there to have a picnic or fly a kite?" I asked.

"No, we couldn't," said Mama.

"We wouldn't have been welcome there," said Daddy.

"That's terrible," I said.

"Yes, it was," Mama said. "It was segregation—keeping people apart because of their race."

"Treating people differently because of the color of their skin," Daddy added.

"What about the Golden Rule?" I asked. "What about treating other people the way you want to be treated?"

"I guess some people forgot that the Golden Rule is supposed to include everyone," said Mama.

For a long time, black and white kids couldn't do many things together. They couldn't go to the same schools or to the same restaurants and libraries or even sit together at the movies. It was the law.

"Why didn't somebody do something about those kinds of laws?" I asked.

"They did," said Mama.

"We did," said Daddy.

Many people—both blacks and whites—knew that segregation was unfair and just plain wrong.

Some people said, *Just wait. Times will change.*

But others said, *Why wait? What's wrong with now?* They held protests at restaurants, stores, and movie theaters. They tried to get officials and courts to make new laws to create a better city—a place that would welcome and include all people.

By the time I was born, some unfair laws had changed in Baltimore. Kids could go to the same schools and libraries, restaurants, and some movie theaters, too—no matter the color of their skin.

"But the amusement park just wouldn't budge," said Daddy.

People who were fed up with segregation made plans to hold a huge protest at the amusement park. They spread the word to churches, synagogues, schools, and other places in the community, so that many people could take part in the protest. They invited newspapers and television stations to report on the protest. They told the police chief about their plans, so the police could keep the peace.

"Best of all, they picked a perfect summer day for the big event—a day when people celebrate what's best about America," said Mama. "What day do you think they chose?"

"The Fourth of July!" I said.

"That's right! A day that stands for freedom," said Mama.

"Did they have fireworks?" I asked.

"They had something even better. Hundreds of people—black and white, young and old, students, teachers, priests, ministers, and rabbis—all came together on July 4, 1963, to take part in one of the biggest protests the city ever had," said Daddy.

"They believed in the Golden Rule—that being fair is the right thing to do," said Mama.

First the protestors went to a church to pray, sing freedom songs, and get ready. They spent the morning learning how to be peaceful protestors—how not to use their fists to fight back. Then they climbed onto buses to go to the amusement park. They brought signs and banners that declared their message of fairness for all.

When the protestors reached the park, a crowd of
angry faces greeted them—people who didn't want
the park to change. They shouted insults at the
protestors.

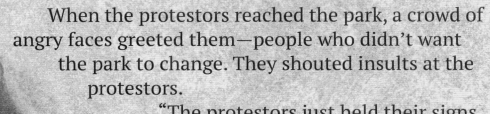

"The protestors just held their signs
high and sang freedom songs. 'We Shall
Overcome'—the civil rights anthem—filled
the air," said Daddy.

"But when they tried to go into the
park to buy tickets—blacks and whites
together—the park's owners had the
protestors arrested," said Mama. "So
they did what they had been taught
to do—to protest peacefully. Some
sat down on the ground and
refused to move. Police
officers had to carry them
to buses to take them to
the police station."

Mama and Daddy
explained that almost
three hundred protestors
were arrested that day.
Some paid a fine and could
go home. But half refused
to pay their fines. They chose
to spend the night in jail instead.
When they went home the next day,
they began planning another protest
for two days later, on July 7.

"Kids helped, too," Mama said.

A newspaper reporter even asked eleven-year-old Lydia Phinney and her aunt Mabel Grant to go on a secret protest at the park. They both had light-colored skin. He thought the park's ticket taker might not know they were black.

On the morning of the second protest, Lydia and her aunt walked up to the ticket booth. They bought tickets and walked right in! They could have been arrested if anyone found out who they were, but nobody noticed. They stayed for two hours and went on some rides, including the carousel. When they left, the protestors weren't there yet, but the reporter was. He interviewed them and wrote about their visit to show what a mistake it is to judge people by the color of their skin.

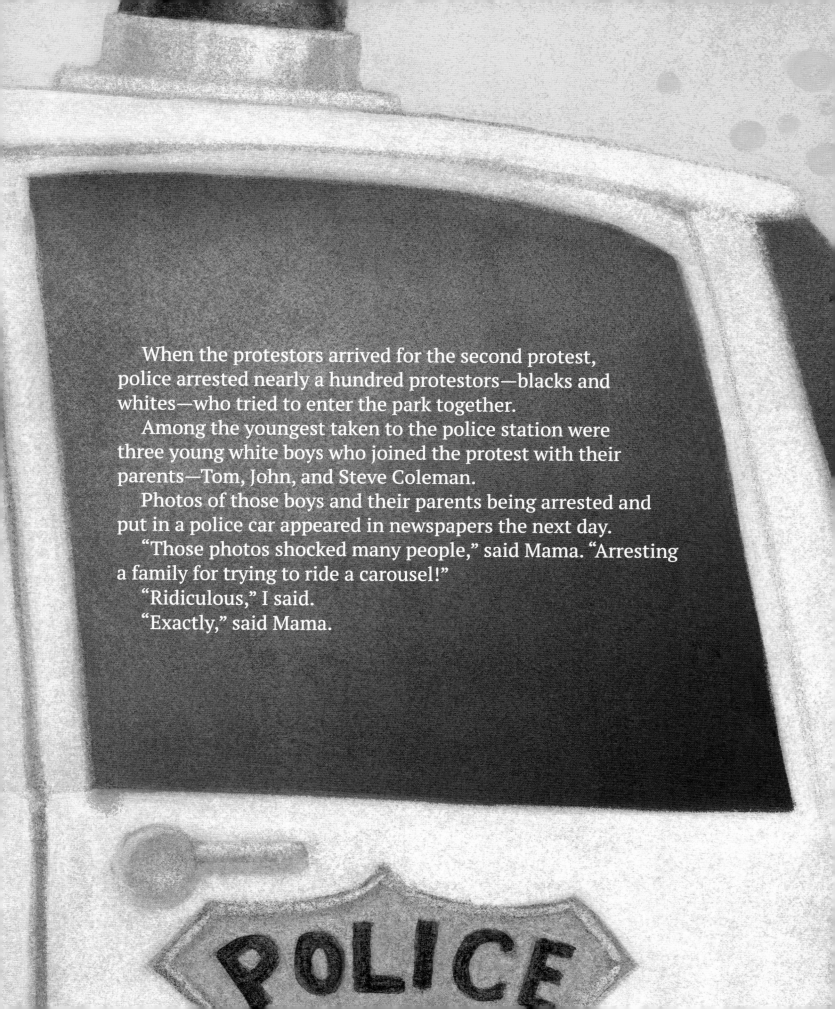

When the protestors arrived for the second protest, police arrested nearly a hundred protestors—blacks and whites—who tried to enter the park together.

Among the youngest taken to the police station were three young white boys who joined the protest with their parents—Tom, John, and Steve Coleman.

Photos of those boys and their parents being arrested and put in a police car appeared in newspapers the next day.

"Those photos shocked many people," said Mama. "Arresting a family for trying to ride a carousel!"

"Ridiculous," I said.

"Exactly," said Mama.

POLICE

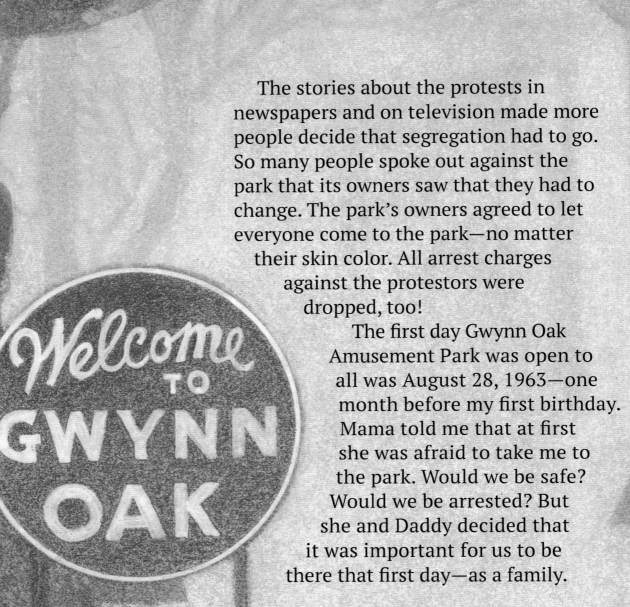

The stories about the protests in newspapers and on television made more people decide that segregation had to go. So many people spoke out against the park that its owners saw that they had to change. The park's owners agreed to let everyone come to the park—no matter their skin color. All arrest charges against the protestors were dropped, too!

The first day Gwynn Oak Amusement Park was open to all was August 28, 1963—one month before my first birthday. Mama told me that at first she was afraid to take me to the park. Would we be safe? Would we be arrested? But she and Daddy decided that it was important for us to be there that first day—as a family.

On August 28, 1963, we were the first African American family to walk into Gwynn Oak Amusement Park when it was open to all.

No angry faces greeted us, only smiling news reporters and photographers, who rushed around us. Daddy said he marched me straight over to the carousel. He helped me onto a big, smiling horse. He put his arm around me and held my hand, so I wouldn't be afraid. Mama stood nearby, waving.

Photographers jumped onto the ride with us. They took photos of Daddy and me, because I was the first African American child to go on a ride that day.

Before the carousel started turning, white kids climbed onto the horses beside me. They were big kids and could probably ride by themselves. But one girl's mother asked Daddy to keep an eye on her daughter, to make sure she didn't fall off her horse. Daddy was glad to help. He kept watch on all us kids, keeping all of us safe.

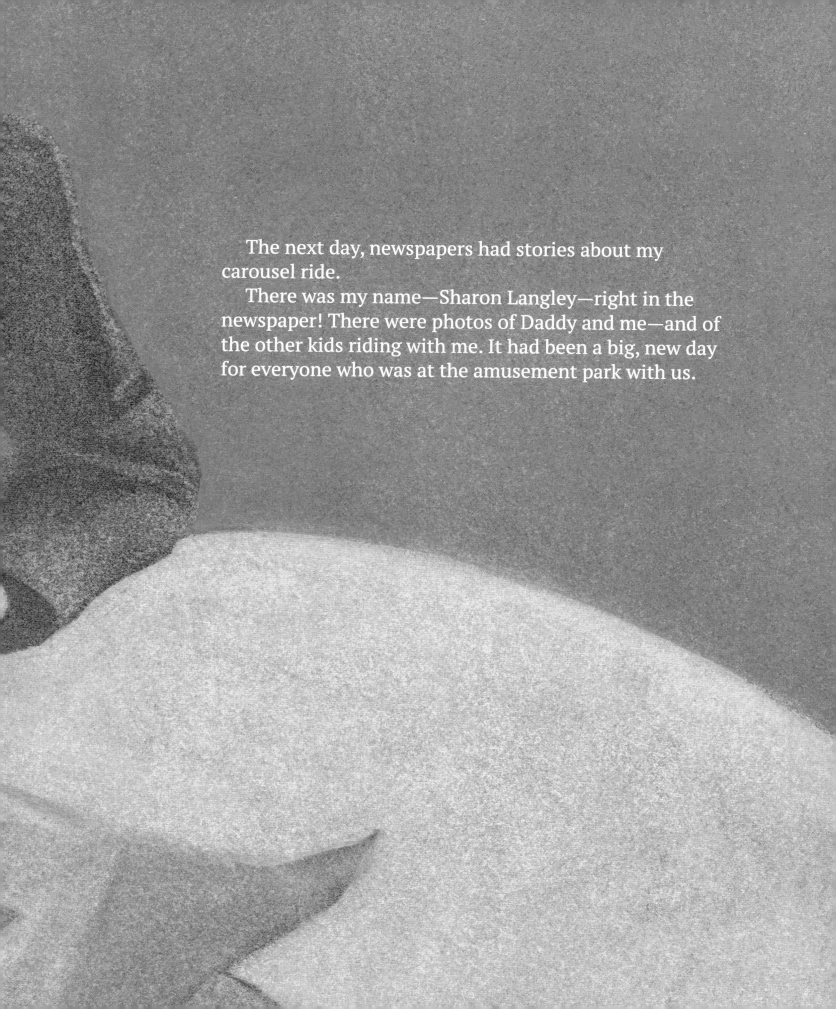

The next day, newspapers had stories about my carousel ride.

There was my name—Sharon Langley—right in the newspaper! There were photos of Daddy and me—and of the other kids riding with me. It had been a big, new day for everyone who was at the amusement park with us.

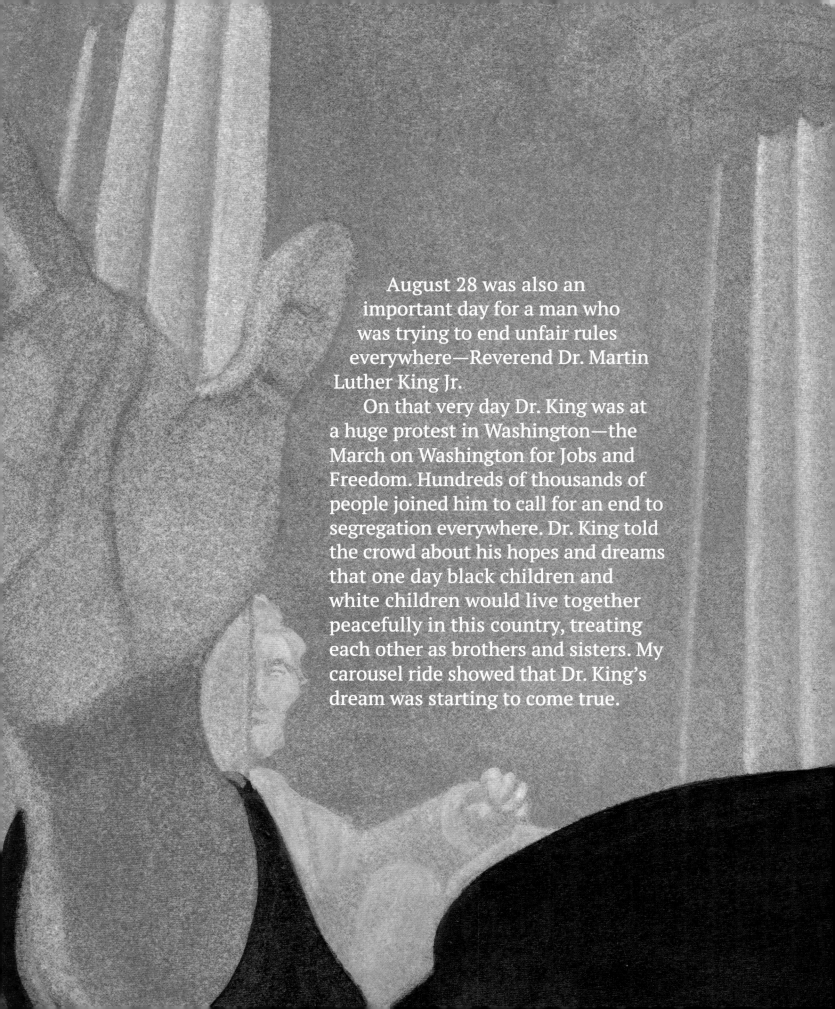

August 28 was also an important day for a man who was trying to end unfair rules everywhere—Reverend Dr. Martin Luther King Jr.

On that very day Dr. King was at a huge protest in Washington—the March on Washington for Jobs and Freedom. Hundreds of thousands of people joined him to call for an end to segregation everywhere. Dr. King told the crowd about his hopes and dreams that one day black children and white children would live together peacefully in this country, treating each other as brothers and sisters. My carousel ride showed that Dr. King's dream was starting to come true.

That was a long time ago. The amusement park isn't there anymore. A big storm destroyed many of the rides and Gwynn Oak Amusement Park had to close. Now it's a park where families have picnics on sunny afternoons and where neighborhood kids play ball. On its green, grassy field stands a sign to help people remember those who took a stand for justice there.

The carousel came through the storm just fine and was moved to Washington, DC, on the National Mall. It's fitting that it should be there, near the monuments that stand for freedom—not far from the Lincoln Memorial where Reverend Dr. Martin Luther King Jr. stood to give his famous speech during the March on Washington.

My name—Sharon Langley—was put on one horse's saddle and on one of its horseshoes, too. A sign on the carousel's fence tells about my ride to remember on that sunny August day so long ago.

Today big kids, little kids, young kids, old kids—no matter the color of their skin—can ride on any carousel, going round and round on horses painted all the colors of the rainbow.

Nobody first and nobody last, everyone equal, having fun together.

A NOTE FROM SHARON LANGLEY

Fifty years after I took my ride, I came to Washington to visit the carousel. I had cousins, aunts, uncles, and other family members there with me. What a thrill to sit on the same horse I rode as a little girl! I was disappointed that my parents couldn't enjoy the celebration with me, but I was so proud of them and the

© Hearst Communications, Inc.

Sharon Langley and her father, Charles C. Langley Jr., at Gwynn Oak Park on August 28, 1963

example of courage and conviction they set for me. They had shown me that everyone—including children—can play a part in creating a world where all are welcome and treated fairly. I imagined that my parents were on the carousel with me, and that my grandparents were there, too. My grandmother had kept the newspaper story about my carousel ride neatly tucked in her Bible, the book that inspires us to follow the Golden Rule—do for others what you'd want them to do for you.

I thought about the hundreds of people who came to the protest fifty years earlier at the Baltimore amusement park. I imagined some of them were riding on these colorful horses, too. And I thought about Reverend Dr. Martin Luther King Jr. and the thousands who worked with him for so many years to end unfair rules everywhere. I envisioned some of them also on the carousel with me. I was glad that many people had stood up for what's right, so that kids today can ride this carousel—and every other carousel, too.

MORE ABOUT THE STORY

The Gwynn Oak ride—renamed the Carousel on the Mall—has been near the Smithsonian museums on the National Mall in Washington, DC, since 1981. A book Amy Nathan wrote for teens and adults—*Round and Round Together: Taking a Merry-Go-Round Ride into the Civil Rights Movement* (2011)—told for the first time

of the link between the Carousel on the Mall, civil rights protests, and the March on Washington. In 2013, for the fiftieth anniversary of the March on Washington, a historical marker was installed at the carousel that briefly tells about Sharon Langley's ride. The horse she rode in 1963 was decorated with the names of civil rights heroes; her name was inscribed on one horseshoe and on a brass plate on the saddle.

This carousel arrived brand-new in 1947 at Baltimore's Gwynn Oak Amusement Park, which had been

© Amy Nathan

Sharon Langley and her extended family at the Carousel on the Mall in 2014 for a family reunion

Sharon Langley with the same horse she rode as a small child

whites-only since it opened in 1894. From 1955 to 1962 small, annual protests against segregation occurred at Gwynn Oak but failed to change the policy. In 1963 Baltimore's chapter of CORE (Congress of Racial Equality) tried a new approach: mass arrests and massive publicity. During two days of nonviolent protests at Gwynn Oak on July 4 and 7, 1963, nearly four hundred people were arrested, among them more than twenty priests, rabbis, and ministers—a first for the civil rights movement. Local and national newspapers showed photos of the arrests of prominent clergy and others, including Johns Hopkins University sociology professor Dr. James S. Coleman, his wife, Lucille, and their three young sons. Negotiations led to the park ending its whites-only policy on August 28, 1963. In 1972 Gwynn Oak Park closed, devastated by Hurricane Agnes. Where it once stood is now a public recreation area. The carousel was sold to the concessionaire for the Smithsonian and installed on the National Mall in 1981.

In July 2013 Sharon Langley came to Baltimore for a fiftieth anniversary commemoration of the end of segregation at Gwynn Oak. She also visited the carousel in Washington that summer and the next with family members. She has followed the example of activism set by her late parents, Charles and Marian Langley. Her mother, as a teenager in the 1950s, helped end segregation at the high school in her hometown—Georgetown, Kentucky. Over the years, Sharon Langley has participated in many civil rights demonstrations and has shown her commitment to creating a more just world as an educator in public schools in Los Angeles, where she has served as a teacher, instructional coach, staff development trainer, and school administrator.

As for other children mentioned in the book, Lydia (Phinney) Wilkins made standing up for equal rights her career, as a program analyst in the Office of Equal Employment Opportunity and Civil Rights. Her aunt, the late Mabel (Grant) Young, a teacher and doctor's wife, had been approached in July 1963 by reporters of the *Baltimore Afro-American* (the *AFRO*) newspaper to go on the undercover mission at Gwynn Oak with her niece on the day of the second protest, thinking that the ticket taker would be too distracted with worries about the upcoming demonstration to look at them closely. An article about their visit appeared in the newspaper on July 9, 1963. Of the Coleman brothers: Tom became an investment banker and university lecturer, John works for Chippewa tribes on environmental issues, and Steve does education research. There is more about the protestors in *Round and Round Together*.

TIMELINE

1894	Gwynn Oak Amusement Park opens as a segregated, whites-only park.
1896	Plessy v. Ferguson: Supreme Court decision upholding the rights of states to pass laws allowing or requiring racial segregation in public and private places.
1947	New carousel arrives at segregated Gwynn Oak Amusement Park.
1954	Brown v. Board of Education: Supreme Court decision against school segregation. Baltimore is one of the first Southern cities to officially end segregation in its schools.
1955	Protests against segregation at Gwynn Oak Park begin—usually small, just once a year.
1962	Baltimore City Council passes a law against segregation in hotels and restaurants.
1963	July 4 and 7: Two big protests at Gwynn Oak Park.
	August 28: Gwynn Oak's first day without segregation. Sharon Langley takes a carousel ride at Gwynn Oak.
	Reverend Dr. Martin Luther King Jr. delivers his "I Have a Dream Speech" at the March on Washington for Jobs and Freedom.
1964	Congress passes the Civil Rights Act ending segregation at all places that serve the public.
1965	Congress passes the Voting Rights Act.
1968	Reverend Dr. Martin Luther King Jr. is killed.
1972	Hurricane damage causes Gwynn Oak Amusement Park to close.
1981	Gwynn Oak Park's carousel moves to Washington, DC.
2013	A Baltimore ceremony on the fiftieth anniversary of the end of segregation at Gwynn Oak.
	Historical markers installed at the carousel in Washington and at the park where Gwynn Oak Amusement Park used to be.

BIBLIOGRAPHY

Events and situations described in *A Ride to Remember* that occurred before 2011 are based in part on the book *Round and Round Together,* which was published in 2011, as well as on the personal recollections of Sharon Langley. *Round and Round Together* has an extensive bibliography of books and articles on the civil rights movement from the 1930s through the mid-1960s in Baltimore and elsewhere; a few of its major sources are listed here, including citations for 1963 newspaper reports. Situations and events described in *A Ride to Remember* that occurred after 2011 are based on the personal recollections of both authors; the articles suggested from 2013 provide more information on the post-2011 events.

BOOKS

Mills, Barbara. *Got My Mind Set on Freedom: Maryland's Story of Black and White Activism 1663–2000.* Westminster, MD: Heritage Books, 2007.

Nathan, Amy. *Round and Round Together: Taking a Merry-Go-Round Ride into the Civil Rights Movement.* Philadelphia: Paul Dry Books, 2011.

Sidney Hollander Foundation. *Toward Equality: Baltimore's Progress Report.* Baltimore: Maryland Historical Society, 2003.

Smith, C. Fraser. *Here Lies Jim Crow: Civil Rights in Maryland.* Baltimore: Johns Hopkins University Press, 2008

ARTICLES

"283 Integrationists, Many Clerics, Are Arrested at Gwynn Oak Park," *Baltimore Sun*, July 5, 1963.

"About 100 Get Arrested at Gwynn Oak," *Baltimore Sun*, July 8, 1963.

"Dr. Blake Among 283 Held in Racial Rally in Maryland," *New York Times*, July 5, 1963.

Franklin, Ben A. "99 Seized in New Demonstration at Segregated Maryland Resort," *New York Times*, July 8, 1963.

"Gwynn Oak Park Integrates Quietly," *Baltimore Afro-American*, August 31, 1963.

"Gwynn Oak Says 'Not Today' as More than 280 Are Jailed," *Baltimore Afro-American*, July 6, 1963.

Langley, Sharon. "Why I Marched on Forsyth County," *Atlanta Voice 21*, no. 24 (February 7–13, 1987).

Mirabella, Lorraine. "50 Years Later, Desegregation of Gwynn Oak Amusement Park Celebrated," *Baltimore Sun,* July 7, 2013.

Nathan, Amy. "The March and the Merry-Go-Round," *Washington Post,* August 23, 2013.

Nathan, Amy. "Gwynn Oak Amusement Park Protest Movement," Oxford African American Studies Center (2013). Available online at www.oxfordaasc.com.

"Negro Family Integrates Gwynn Oak in Brief Visit," *Baltimore Sun,* August 29, 1963.

"Park at Baltimore Integrates Quietly," *New York Times,* August 29, 1963.

Williams, James D. "2 Integrate Gwynn Oak While 95 are Arrested," *Baltimore Afro-American,* July 9, 1963. (This article misnames the eleven-year-old at the park on July 7, 1963, calling her "Pauline," a name others in her family had; she was known then as Lydia Phinney and is now Lydia Wilkins.)

ACKNOWLEDGMENTS

Sharon and Amy both grew up in Baltimore, although we met only as adults. Amy, who lived not far from Gwynn Oak Amusement Park as a child, learned in 2008 about Sharon's famous 1963 carousel ride from a brief mention in *Here Lies Jim Crow* by C. Fraser Smith. Amy's research uncovered something no book, including Smith's, had reported—that the park's carousel had moved to the National Mall in Washington, DC. Amy first spoke with Sharon in 2009, interviewing her by phone for the book that Amy then wrote for teens and adults, *Round and Round Together.* Warm thanks go to all who were interviewed for that book and to its publisher, Paul Dry. It set the stage for this new picture book, a joyful collaboration between Sharon and Amy involving all aspects of the planning and writing process, a coming together that mirrors the coming together that led to the end of segregation at Gwynn Oak Park. We are so glad to have come to know the Hunter family—Donna, Bruce, and the late Stan Hunter—concessionaires for the Smithsonian. We appreciate how they, Smithsonian Enterprises, and the National Park Service have embraced their carousel's civil rights legacy. Thanks also go to both of our extended families for their encouragement and support. In addition we are very grateful to our agents, Christine LeBlond and Susan Schulman; to our editor, Howard Reeves; to our illustrator, Floyd Cooper; and also to Emily Daluga and the Abrams creative team for giving this story such a warm reception.

For my parents—your lessons of courage and
compassion continue to guide my life
—SL

For all who have the courage to stand up
and speak out against injustice
—AN

For Pop Pop's buddy, NIKO!
—FC

The artwork for this book was created using oil erasure on illustration board.

Cataloging-in-Publication Data has been applied for and may be obtained from the Library of Congress.
ISBN 978-1-4197-3685-8

Printed and bound in China
10 9 8 7 6 5 4 3 2 1

Abrams Books for Young Readers are available at special discounts when purchased in quantity for premiums
and promotions as well as fundraising or educational use. Special editions can also be created to specification.
For details, contact specialsales@abramsbooks.com or the address below.
Abrams® is a registered trademark of Harry N. Abrams, Inc.

ABRAMS The Art of Books
195 Broadway, New York, NY 10007
abramsbooks.com